MW00637598

THE·FALL
OF THE AZTEC
EMPIRE

THE·FALL OF THE AZTEC EMPIRE

FOREWORD
H. B. NICHOLSON

ESSAY BY
JANE STEVENSON DAY

THE DRAWINGS OF
KEITH HENDERSON

DENVER MUSEUM OF NATURAL HISTORY
ROBERTS RINEHART PUBLISHERS

1993

CARLYE C. WATTIS GENEROUSLY CONTRIBUTED
TO THE PUBLICATION OF THIS BOOK.

The Denver Museum of Natural History gratefully acknowledges
Chatto & Windus Publishers, London, for granting permission to reproduce
Keith Henderson's drawings. We also thank Dr. Peter Knox-Shaw, Keith Henderson's nephew,
for his encouragement in this project, and Dr. Patricia Anawalt,
for providing us with our first glimpse of Henderson's drawings.

Copyright © 1993 Denver Museum of Natural History
All Rights Reserved

Book Design: Ann W. Douden
Maps: Jackie MacFarland and Laura Malick
Art Production: Jackie MacFarland, Danielle Okin, and Lori Williamson

Published in the United States of America by
Roberts Rinehart Publishers, Post Office Box 666, Niwot, Colorado 80544

Published in Great Britain, Ireland, and Europe by
Roberts Rinehart Publishers,
Main Street, Schull, West Cork
Republic of Ireland

Library of Congress Catalog Card Number 93-84166
International Standard Book Number 1-879373-43-2

Manufactured in the United States of America

CONTENTS

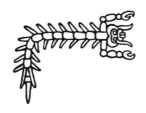

FOREWORD

I am not sure when I first discovered, with wonder, excitement, and delight, the 1934 edition of William H. Prescott's *The Conquest of Mexico*. I am certain, though, that it was in the branch of the San Diego Public Library that was housed in Florence Elementary School, located in the Hillcrest district of San Diego, California. I graduated from Florence in early 1937, age eleven. In the sixth grade, my most memorable teacher was Harlan Wilson, then a recent graduate of San Diego State College (whose athletic teams were known as the Aztecs). He was interested in Aztec and Maya civilizations, and lent me a little book, *The Aztecs*, by A. Van Doren Honeyman, published in 1905 in a series entitled "Library of the Great World." This book aroused in me a strong, continuing fascination with ancient Mexico.

It was my earlier encounter with the 1934 Prescott, however, that initially sparked my interest. This classic derived from the 1922 edition—the first to include a wealth of pen-and-ink illustrations by the distinguished British artist, Keith Henderson. I well remember my doting on this volume, checking it out innumerable times and tracing many of its illustrations, especially those taken from the codices. I still have these tracings. The Van Doren Honeyman book had only one illustration, a photograph of the "Sacrificial Stone" (Cuauhxicalli of Tizoc), so the Henderson illustrations constituted my first real introduction to the splendor of Prehispanic Mesoamerican art—and I reveled in them. Along with a few other influences—particularly my frequent visits to the great rotunda of the San Diego Museum of Man, in Balboa Park, which featured casts of the Quirigua stelae and giant zoomorphs and the Carlos Vierra murals of six of the most important Lowland Maya ruins—the Henderson illustrations so fired my youthful imagination that, looking back, my eventual career in the field of Mesoamerican studies seems to have been almost predestined.

Keith Henderson enjoyed a remarkably long and successful career as an artist and illustrator. In preparation for his Prescott project, he assiduously studied the relevant literature and artifacts available in the British Museum. He was most aided by T. A. Joyce, who in 1914 had published his influential *Mexican Archaeology*. Henderson's illustrations are particularly strong on costume, civil and military, on both the native Mexican and European sides. He was especially impressed with the skilled draftsmanship of the artists who illustrated the ritual-divinatory screenfolds that can be assigned to the Mixteca-Puebla stylistic-iconographic tradition (Codices Borgia, Vaticanus B, Cospi, Laud, Fejérváry-Mayer, Zouche-Nuttall, Vindobonensis, et al.), and he copied many images from them. As Joyce noted in his introduction, these are not "Aztec" in the narrower sense, but they do exemplify traditions that were contemporary and that may hail from areas subject to the political control of Mexico Tenochtitlan. Henderson used to good advantage the "Aztec" pictorial par excellence, the Codex Mendoza. Unfortunately, he does not seem to have had access to a reproduction of the Codex Borbonicus, the classic "Aztec"-style ritual-divinatory screenfold, which would have provided him with more accurate illustrations of the deities and rituals of the imperial capital and its neighborhood.

In spite of his exceptionally conscientious research, Keith Henderson made some mistakes. But the overall achievement of this gifted artist, born during the height of Queen Victoria's reign, was remarkable. Certainly no one before or since has visually captured more successfully the drama and color of one of the most epic cultural and military confrontations in world history.

H. B. NICHOLSON, PH.D.
EMERITUS PROFESSOR OF ANTHROPOLOGY
UNIVERSITY OF CALIFORNIA, LOS ANGELES

Preface

William H. Prescott's seminal history, *The Conquest of Mexico*, was first published in 1843 and has been reprinted many times since. The 1922 edition, published in Great Britain by Chatto & Windus Publishers and in the United States by Henry Holt & Company, contained magnificent drawings by Keith Henderson, a well-known British artist, writer, and intellectual of his day. For the 1922 edition, Henderson produced illustrations of amazing precision and quality. The stark strength and simplicity of his drawings have stimulated the imagination of all who have seen them.

Henderson was born in Scotland in 1883. He lived to be almost one hundred years old and remained a prolific artist until his death in South Africa in 1982. He was part of an extraordinary generation of illustrators born toward the end of the nineteenth century that included such well known figures as Edmond Dulac and Max Armfield. Educated at Marlborough College, Henderson studied art at the Slade School in London and Academie de la Grande Chaumière in Paris. Although he was best known in the art world as a painter in oils and watercolors, throughout his life he combined his artistic talent with a love of literature. This led him to produce many beautiful sets of paintings and drawings for books.

While serving in the cavalry in World War I, Henderson read Prescott's *The Conquest of Mexico* and was so impressed by it that he became determined to create illustrations for a two-volume edition of the book. After the war, he spent a year doing painstaking research in the collections of the British Museum, preparing himself for the endeavor that would be his finest published achievement. Each completed drawing was carefully inspected for authenticity by members of the museum's professional archaeological staff before Henderson would approve it for the book. Finally, in 1922, over two hundred of his magnificent pen-and-ink drawings were published to great acclaim.

Published just once more, in 1934, by the Junior Literary Guild in New York, the Henderson editions have long been out of print. Most readers of Prescott's incredible story of the encounter of the Spanish and the Aztecs in Mexico have seen either earlier editions with dated lithographs or more modern versions with no illustrations. While over the ensuing years our knowledge of Aztec culture has greatly increased, the aim of this book is not to rewrite Prescott's volume but rather to share again with a new audience Henderson's splendid drawings, whose liveliness and creativity still bring to life the incredible story of the fall of the Aztec empire.

JANE STEVENSON DAY, PH.D.
CHIEF CURATOR
DENVER MUSEUM OF NATURAL HISTORY

Artist's Preface

This edition is the outcome of an obsession, a certainty that when at last the World War should come to an end I must make a picture-book of *The Conquest of Mexico*. With conquest in the air, soldiering an all too familiar trade, religions in the melting-pot, and on the horizon a romantic brightness, this book seemed to me like the ship in which I would sail away to undiscovered islands.

From the outset, however, it was evident that the charm of such an adventure might be complicated by the necessity for an unusual amount of archaeological impedimenta, my objective being ancient Mexico, not modern Mexico. The old Gods have fled that country, and now one finds some of them, sitting in ghostly quiet in the British Museum.

There, when I went to apply for further information, the authorities were so astonishingly kind that at first I thought I must have been mistaken for some important personage. But no. Such courtesy is "the tradition" apparently. Mr. T. A. Joyce, the high-priest, gave me a table to work at, while from cupboards and cases the treasures of ancient Mexico (their very curves a shock of lovely surprise) one by one were brought out to be studied at leisure, as well as books such as the Codex Zouche, the Codex Borgia, the Codex Laud, the Codex Fejérváry-Mayer—superb pictorial achievements that every art student ought to investigate. There are no barriers, no unreasonable restrictions, and Mr. Joyce never seems to get tired of answering questions. Yet for all he has taught me, for all those generous hours, I have only gratitude to offer in return. Here, also, I would thank Lord Cowdray, Miss L. E. Elliott, Mr. Alfred Maudslay, Mr. Russell Cairns, Mr. T. A. Sprague, Mr. W. P. Pycraft, and Mr. Julian Huxley for the help they have given in various ways. As to the illustrations themselves, it may be noted that from the time when, in the story, the Europeans arrive in Mexico, I imagine myself as having arrived with them—as a spy to begin with and eventually a deserter.

In the following list of illustrations [found in this edition on page 116] there are a number of references to the Codices, to early Spanish Chroniclers, and other sources. These I have included, in order that purely archaeological details may easily be verified, and their value not confused with the aesthetic intention—which is, of course, the main issue.

KEITH HENDERSON

(reprinted with permission from the 1922 edition of *The Conquest of Mexico*,
published by Chatto & Windus, London)

PART I

THE FALL OF THE AZTEC EMPIRE

JANE STEVENSON DAY

SPAIN AND THE CONQUISTADORES

In 1469, the marriage of Ferdinand of Aragon and Isabella of Castile united Spain for the first time in eight hundred years. Under the joint reign of these monarchs, the Moors were finally defeated at Granada in 1492, completing the reconquest of Spain from Islam. Marked by this long-sought achievement, 1492 proved to be the most momentous year in Spanish history. Under the urging of Tomas de Torquemada, the Queen's confidant and confessor, the Inquisition was reinstalled in the Iberian Peninsula; an edict was issued expelling the Jews from Spain and prohibiting their settlement in Spanish-held territories. And, after six frustrating years of waiting around the periphery of the court, Christopher Columbus was finally given royal permission to sail westward in search of a shortcut to the riches of the Indies.

The conquistadores who followed in the footsteps of Columbus were unique products of Spanish history. As a breed of men they were not new to Spain;

indeed they had comprised an essential part of her culture since A.D. 711. In that year Islamic hordes from north Africa swept across the Strait of Gibraltar to conquer, within seven years, all but Spain's northwest coastal region. The Moors marched through the Pyrenees into France, where they were finally stopped by the Franks. The Moors conquered with the sword in the name of the Prophet Mohammed. But, along with terror and bloodshed, they also brought to Spain the rich culture of the Middle East. Their knowledge of irrigation methods made arid lands usable for agriculture, and education, mathematics, science, and the arts flourished at the Moorish courts.

From 711 until 1492 Spain was at war with these Moorish invaders, constantly seeking to return the Iberian Peninsula to Spanish rule. While the rest of Christian Europe marched on crusades to regain the Holy Land, Spaniards battled the infidels on their own doorstep. This incessant struggle for their land and faith left an indelible mark on the Spanish character. Any man of breeding regarded himself a soldier of the cross—a conquistador dedicated to banishing Islam from Spanish soil. However, for hundreds of years Spain lacked the national unity needed to expel the Moors. Not until the reign of the Catholic monarchs Isabella and Ferdinand was

SPAIN

Bay of Biscay

Santiago

KINGDOM OF NAVARRE

Pyrenees

KINGDOM OF CASTILE AND LEON

Duero River

Salamanca

Madrid

KINGDOM OF ARAGON

CATALONIA

N

Balearic Islands

KINGDOM OF PORTUGAL

Tagus River

Caceres

Trujillo

Medellín

Guadiana River

Valencia

Lisbon

ESTREMADURA

Cordoba

Guadalquivir River

Mediterranean Sea

Seville

ANDALUSIA

Baza

Granada

Malaga

Almería

Cadiz

Atlantic Ocean

Strait of Gibralter

AFRICA

Ceuta

unification finally achieved. Under their leadership the Spanish finally drove their Moorish conquerors back into Africa.

Granada was the Moor's last great stronghold. The fall of two other major centers of Arab rule in the south, Malaga and Baza, had weakened the Caliph of Granada's will to resist. The siege of this great fortress city began in April 1491. On January 2, 1492, Granada finally surrendered, and the beautiful capital opened its gates to the victorious armies of Isabella and Ferdinand. Spain was on the threshold of a new period of nationalism and discovery.

This fervent religious crusade of Christian against Moslem had taken eight centuries to complete and had left in its wake unemployed soldiers and nobles who were little more than warlords. These men were born to the saddle and the sword, accustomed to taking booty and living off the land. They were consumed by a religious fervor that had led to victory in the reconquest of their land. When in 1492 the last battles were won, the conquistadores of the Spanish crusade looked for new worlds to conquer. They were men with little to lose and much to gain by adventuring in the footsteps of Columbus.

The conquistadores were not men of gentle nature. They saw themselves as warriors and crusaders, men with a mission to conquer and to baptize, and in the process, acquire gold and glory. Born into a world of racial and religious intolerance, of crusading knights, of war, and of change, the conquistadores believed in the invincibility of Spanish arms and in their own power and ability—characteristics that would serve them well in the Americas, as they advanced with unbelievable self-confidence and brutality against what seemed impossible odds for survival. Accounts of their conquests read like modern fiction; we might have trouble believing them if not for the written documentation so dear to Spanish bureaucracy and the testimony of the indigenous people themselves.

All regions of Spain contributed men to the hordes that flocked to the New World, but the province of Estremadura in western Spain is known as the Cradle of the Conquistadores. Here both Hernán Cortés and Francisco Pizarro were born. And from here, they and other captains bound for the Americas recruited their best men. The area today looks much as it did five hundred years ago. This stark land is characterized by a high inland plateau, with wide vistas and small villages perched on rocky outcrops. Old castles and fortresses still dot the landscape, and the ancient towns where the conquistadores were born still stand.

Cortés

The best known of the Spanish captians who found their way to the Americas was without question Hernán Cortés. Cortés was a man of his times, a soldier of fortune, cruel, proud, adventurous, and overwhelmingly ambitious. But Cortés also had incredible courage and was a born leader. His story dominates the record of the encounter between the Aztecs and Spanish that led to the fall of the Aztec empire.

Hernán Cortés was born in 1485 in the small town of Medellín. His father was Martín Cortés de Monroy and his mother was Doña Catalina Pizarro Altamarino. The family claimed minor nobility, but had little means. At the age of fourteen Cortés was sent to study at the University of Salamanca, one of Europe's earliest universities and, at the time, the most prestigious center of learning in Spain. Accounts vary as to the nature of Cortés's studies, but his later writings and actions suggest he studied law and Latin. After two years, Cortés tired of school and returned home to Medellín, to the annoyance of his parents, who had hoped to see their son trained for a profitable legal career. The two years at Salamanca, along with extensive training and experience as a notary in Cuba and Hispañola, gave Cortés a familiarity with Castilian legal codes that would later help him justify his unauthorized conquest of Mexico.

At this point of his life, Cortés was described by Francisco López de Gómara, his biographer and secretary-chaplin, as restless, haughty, and mischievous—probably a fair description of a teenaged boy who had returned to his small town only to find himself frustrated by provincial life. By this time in 1499 the exciting news of Columbus's discoveries was pouring back to Spain. Cortés and his parents must have been well aware of the possibilities these discoveries presented for an adventurous young man. In 1502 Cortés's father arranged for his son to sail to the Americas with a family acquaintance, Nicolás de Ovando, the newly appointed governor of Hispañola. But Cortés injured himself while hurriedly escaping from the bedroom of a married woman of Medellín and could not make the journey. He considered joining the great Spanish general, Gonsalvo de Cordova, in the Italian wars, but instead probably spent the next year in the heady atmosphere of Spain's southern ports, listening to his compatriots who had returned from the Indies with tales of discovery, conquest, gold, Indians, and exotic lands.

In 1504, at the age of nineteen, Cortés sailed in a convoy of merchant ships bound for Santo Domingo, the capital of Hispañola. Upon his arrival, he registered as a citizen of the colony, which entitled him to a building plot and land for cultivation. Soon after, Ovando, still the governor, gave Cortés a *repartimiento* (an allocation of Indian laborers) and made him a town notary in Azúa. Although the gold he hoped to find was not readily at hand, Cortés spent the next five years establishing himself in the growing colony. During this interlude, evidence suggests that Cortés contracted syphilis through fraternization with local Indian women. Until that time syphilis was unknown in the Old World, but the disease wreaked great havoc there after its introduction.

In 1511 Cortés was sent with Diego Velásquez and three hundred men to conquer Cuba. There, at age twenty-six, Cortés served as clerk to the treasurer, a position that entailed keeping account of the King's "fifth"—that portion of all wealth from the New World designated for the King of Spain. In Cuba, Cortés became a man of importance, with land, mines, and cattle, and became related to Velásquez himself through a rather reluctant marriage to the governor's sister-in-law, Catalina.

After spending almost fifteen years in the Indies, Cortés began to look beyond his substantial status as an *acalde,* or mayor, of the capital of Cuba and a man of means in the thriving colony. By then he was experienced in politics and law and had the financial resources to take advantage of whatever opportunity might come his way. That opportunity finally presented itself toward the end of 1518. In 1517, and again in the early part of 1518, two voyages partly funded by Governor Velásquez were made to the Yucatan Peninsula from western Cuba. The first, the Hernández de Córdoba expedition, brought back gold, idols, and tales of large towns with sophisticated Indian populations. These reports were enough to suggest that in the Yucatan lay the wealth the conquistadores had been dreaming of since the days of Columbus. Velásquez immediately launched another expedition, under the command of Juan de Grijalva, that discovered the island of Cozumel and sailed up the gulf coast of Mexico. Grijalva opened the door to Mexico, but it was Cortés who claimed it.

On October 23, 1518, Velásquez signed an agreement appointing Cortés Captain General of the third expedition. The agreement between the two men stated that the objectives of the voyage were exploration, discovery, and conversion of the natives and their acceptance of Spanish sovereignty. Cortés mortgaged his lands in Cuba and borrowed six thousand gold pesos from the merchants of Santiago—gambling all he owned on the success of the venture. Jealous gossip, possibly justified, suggested to the governor that perhaps he had chosen the wrong man for the command—that Cortés was too ambitious and might take the spoils of the voyage for himself, despite the contract he had signed with Velásquez. Velásquez's suspicions mounted and Cortés, fearing he might be replaced, ordered his ships to sail for the port of Trinidad. There Cortés took on provisions and recruited two hundred of Grijalva's soldiers recently returned from the Yucatán. In Trinidad Cortés also added to his standard some of his greatest captains, including Montejo Sandeval and the four Alvarado brothers, all seasoned veterans.

THE VOYAGE TO MEXICO

On February 23, 1519, Hernán Cortés, at age thirty-four, set sail from Cuba in search of gold, glory, and souls. He was accompanied by 2 priests, 500 soldiers, 50 sailors, 200 islanders from Cuba who served as bearers, several black servants, and a few Indian women. Also on board his 11 ships were 16 horses, 14 pieces of artillery, food supplies, and trinkets and clothing for trading. For its time, the expedition was well equipped and staffed. Under the leadership of Cortés, it was destined to become a disciplined fighting force. In a speech to his men Cortés laid out his dream:

> I offer you great rewards, although they will be wrapped about
> with great hardships. . . . . and if you do not abandon me, as I
> shall not abandon you, I shall make you in a very short time the
> richest of all men who have crossed the seas. . . .[1]

Like Grijalva, Cortés stopped on Cozumel island. There he heard of two Spanish sailors, shipwrecked eight years earlier in a Caribbean storm, who lived on the Yucatan Peninsula. One of them, Jerónimo de Aguilar, was ransomed from his Maya Indian captors to join Cortés's expedition as guide and interpreter. The other chose to remain with his Maya wife and children, and was eventually killed fighting with Indian troops against the Spanish.

From Cozumel, Cortés sailed his ships around the tip of the Yucatan Peninsula and up the gulf coast. Along the way he and his men paused to trade in local Indian towns and heard the natives tell of the powerful Aztecs and their empire rich in gold ruled by the feared emperor Moctezuma II. When the Spanish soldiers stopped for food and water at the town of Potonchán in Tabasco, native forces attacked them.

Cortés mounted a cavalry charge against the Indians, and after a hard-fought battle, with losses on both sides, the Spaniards emerged victorious. The Tabascan *cacique*, or chief, gave Cortés gifts, including twenty young women, all of whom were expeditiously baptized by the expedition's friar Father Bartolomé Olmedo, and shared among the Spanish captains. Among the women was a bright and beautiful young Indian girl baptized as Marina. As a child she was sold into slavery in Tabasco and learned to speak the Maya language. But she had been born in a Nahua-speaking village in eastern Veracruz so she also spoke Nahuatl, the Aztec language. This capability proved to be of crucial importance to the Spanish. Marina became the mistress of Cortés and eventually bore him a son. With her quick wit and language skills she also became Cortés's interpreter of the Aztec language and of its culture as well. She is depicted in the pictorial accounts of the conquest as "the tongue of Cortés," standing between the Spanish captain and his Aztec contacts.

MESOAMERICA

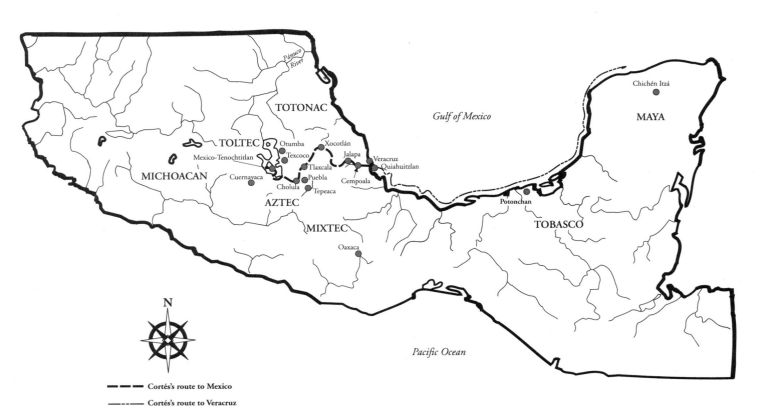

Cortés's route to Mexico

Cortés's route to Veracruz

Sailing northward along the east coast of Mexico, Cortés landed near the site of the modern city of Veracruz. There on the beach, the priest-soldier Father Olmedo gathered the Spanish forces and their newly acquired women. Kneeling in the sand, they offered thanks for their safe arrival. In the European calendar the date was Good Friday, April 22, 1519. In the Aztec calendar, the year was *Ce Acatl*, also called 1 Reed, a momentous date in Aztec legend and history. Five hundred years earlier, in the year 1 Reed, the ancestral god-king Topiltzin Quetzalcoatl, once ruler of the mighty Toltecs, was driven from his throne. With his loyal followers, Quetzalcoatl fled to the Gulf Coast and sailed to the East, promising to return in the year *Ce Acatl* to reclaim his lost kingdom.

THE AZTECS

Like Spain, the Aztec empire was at its height in 1519. The Aztecs, or Mexica as they called themselves (thus the modern name Mexico), were latecomers to the Valley of Mexico, emigrants from the desert frontiers of northern Mesoamerica. Legend says they left their original homeland of Aztlan about A.D. 1100. Led by their tribal god, Huitzilopochtli, they arrived in the central Valley of Mexico around 1200. In 1325 they founded their great capital, Tenochtitlan, where Mexico City stands today. Tenochtitlan was constructed on a rocky island near the edge of a large lake that once filled the Valley.

HUITZILOPOCHTLI

The Aztec way of life was based on a legacy of 3,000 years of Mesoamerican high culture. From earlier civilizations, the Aztecs inherited ancient traditions of urbanism, agriculture, trade routes, markets—and a religion that believed blood sacrifice was necessary to sustain the order of the natural world. Like their predecessors, the Aztecs had no draft animals; nor did they have use of the wheel. Still, they built a great empire that stretched to both coasts and south to Guatemala. Tenochtitlan was the sacred and secular heart of this expanding state. This beautiful city was constructed on a series of artificial islands, with canals for streets, towering pyramids, and splendid public buildings. With a population of at least 250,000, it was one of the largest cities in the world.

The capital could be approached via four major causeways that connected it to the mainland. Along one of these causeways ran an aqueduct carrying fresh water to the city. In this sophisticated metropolis were government buildings, schools, ball-courts, temples, pyramids, palaces, and common residences. At the city's center was the sacred precinct where the gods of the Aztec pantheon were worshipped through song, dance, and ritual sacrifice. At the heart of the precinct stood the Templo Mayor, or Great Temple. This massive double pyramid was dedicated to the Aztecs' two most important gods, Tlaloc, God of Rain, and Huitzilopochtli, God of War and the Sun. These deities were responsible for the sustenance of the Aztec empire. Tlaloc provided for the state's agricultural needs and Huitzilopochtli assured its financial stability through tribute resulting from wars of conquest.

The Spanish were particularly impressed with Tenochtitlan's highly organized administrative system that included courts, judges, and state taxation. They also marveled at the bustling city's enormous markets that boasted a rich variety of products. A local market system supplied the daily needs of the city, while a long-distance trade network provided exotic items for the nobility of Tenochtitlan. This lucrative trade, which took human caravans to distant corners of the Aztec realm, was controlled by the *pochteca*, a group of rich and powerful merchants.

PARROT

In addition to trade goods, wealth flowed into Tenochtitlan as tribute from conquest. Successful warfare extended the boundaries of the state and also forced conquered towns to supply the emperor with highly valued materials, including colorful tropical bird feathers, fine cotton cloth, jade, gold, jewels, cacao beans (chocolate), and humans destined for sacrifice to the ever demanding Aztec gods. This tribute system was overseen by the feared and hated state tribute collectors whose authority was backed by powerful Aztec armies.

Aztec society was divided into strictly delineated social strata. At the apex of the hierarchy, a powerful and privileged noble class controlled the empire's wealth and labor forces. This upper class provided the state with military leaders, bureaucrats, judges, high priests, teachers, and rulers. The highest position was that of

FISHERMAN

emperor. The office was hereditary within one family, but was often passed to the ruler's brother before his son. Moctezuma II was the nephew of the last emperor and son and grandson of previous rulers.

The largest class in Aztec society was comprised of the commoners, free men and women who formed the backbone of the empire. They served the state as farmers, craftsworkers, and soldiers, but had little opportunity for upward social mobility. In the Aztec system, people were bound to the life and class into which they were born, unless awarded special privileges on the battlefield.

The least fortunate within this rigid system were slaves, who were brought from far corners of the empire by traders to be sold in the marketplace. Many criminals also became slaves. The Aztec system of justice often punished crimes by enslaving the guilty to the aggrieved party. Unlike other parts of the world, slavery was not hereditary and children of slaves were born free.

The Aztecs considered themselves the people of the sun. All males, commoners and nobles alike, were trained as warriors and were on call for military duty. In this role they were responsible for providing sacrificial victims, whose blood was required to sustain the sun in its daily journey across the sky. This need to maintain the cosmos, or else perish, was the basis for the warrior cult of the Aztec state. This cult promoted warfare as the means for taking prisoners to be offered on the sacrificial stone of the Templo Mayor. Their blood provided sustenance for the sun and another day of life and light for the world.

Although the empire focused on war, the Aztecs were also sensitive scholars, artists, and poets. In Tenochtitlan, stone sculptors brilliantly carved massive blocks of volcanic stone; scholars and teachers were greatly honored. Even warriors and kings were poets, reflecting in powerful metaphor the eternal themes of war and glory:

> Proud of itself
> is the city of Mexico-Tenochtitlan.
> Here no one fears to die in war.
> This is our glory
> . . . .
> Have this in mind, oh princes,
> do not forget it.
> Who could conquer Tenochtitlan?
> Who could shake the foundation of heaven?[2]

From its great capital at Tenochtitlan, the sixteenth-century Aztec state dominated much of Mesoamerica. Yet, in spite of its size and power, it was not a truly unified nation. In reality it was an economic empire formed of vanquished provinces that were forced to continuously supply their Aztec masters with tribute. Military superiority established the Aztecs' rights to the wealth of conquered cities and provinces. This imposition of heavy tribute left bitterness and resentment in its wake. Cortés would use this smoldering resentment to his advantage, enlisting native allies to help him conquer the great city of Tenochtitlan.

MOCTEZUMA II

MOCTEZUMA II

Moctezuma II, or Moctezuma Xocoyotzin (the younger), was the last great Aztec emperor. Born in 1467, he grew up during the most glorious years of the Aztec empire, when the city of Tenochtitlan was at its height of power. Trained, like all Aztec rulers, as both a priest and a warrior, Moctezuma was one of the empire's two highest military commanders when he was chosen emperor in 1502.

From 1502 until his death during the battle for Tenochtitlan in 1520, Moctezuma Xocoyotzin was the absolute ruler of the powerful Aztec state. During his reign he led major military expeditions, put down rebellions, and attempted to confirm and solidify the borders of the empire. He imposed heavy taxes upon his subjects both at home and in the conquered provinces, constantly increasing the levy of tribute in both labor and goods.

Moctezuma lived in sumptuous luxury in a splendid palace at the heart of Tenochtitlan, where he was served by thousands of retainers. His many wives and concubines, with their numerous children, lived in special quarters within the palace. The emperor's clothing was made of the finest cotton decorated with colorful designs and he wore magnificent jewelry of jade, gold, and precious stones. Moctezuma's elaborate meals included foods brought from all regions of the empire. He was served a wonderful variety of native New World produce such as corn, tomatoes, avocados, beans, chilies, squash, sweet potatoes, and peanuts as well as fruits imported from the hot tropical lowlands. This diverse menu was supplemented by protein from wild game and fish and domesticated turkeys and dogs. The meal ended with a rich drink of frothing chocolate served in a golden cup. Musicians and dancers provided entertainment while the great ruler dined and smoked a tube of native tobacco before retiring.

Living in isolated splendor, Moctezuma was regarded as semidivine by his people. As such, he was both feared and respected. He governed as mighty warrior, high priest, stern father, and the embodiment of the god of kings, Tezcatlipoca—a deity conceived as an all-powerful, handsome warrior, ever young and virile. In his physical appearance, comportment, and accomplishments, Moctezuma was the ideal symbol of the wealth, sophistication, and strength of the Aztec empire.

Our only description of the emperor is in the words of Bernal Díaz del Castillo, one of Cortés's soldiers:

> The great [Moctezuma] was about forty years old, of good height, well proportioned, spare and slight . . . He did not wear his hair long but just over his ears, and he had a short black beard, well-shaped and thin. His face was rather long and cheerful, he had fine eyes, and in his appearance and manner could express geniality or, when necessary, a serious composure. . . . He had many women as his mistresses, the daughters of chieftains, but two legitimate wives who were *Caciques* in their own right. . .[3]

Moctezuma's fate was to be interwoven with that of the Spanish captain Hernán Cortés. Their encounter in the Americas in the early sixteenth century is one of the most dramatic and astounding events in the history of the world.

The Great Encounter

SCRIBE

From Cortés's first contacts on the mainland of Mexico, Aztec observers continuously monitored his ship's progress and sent regular reports to Moctezuma. Specially trained artist-scribes sketched the likenesses of Cortés and his captains. They also drew images of the horses and the large mastiff dogs that accompa-

HORSE

nied the Spanish, animals unknown in the Americas. Swift runners then transported these drawings to the palace in Tenochtitlan. As soon as the Spanish landed at Veracruz, messengers carried word of their arrival to the emperor, who then dispatched ambassadors to greet the Spanish with elaborate gifts:

> The first was a disk in the shape of the sun, as big as a cartwheel and made of very fine gold. . . . a marvelous thing . . . There was another larger disk of brightly shining silver in the shape of the moon . . . Next they brought crests of gold, plumes of rich green feathers, silver crests, some fans of the same material, models of deer in hollow gold . . . and thirty loads of beautiful cotton cloth . . .[4]

In addition to these treasures, the ambassadors brought the garments and turquoise mask of the god Quetzalcoatl and dressed Cortés in the magnificent costume.

Cortés's arrival in Mexico in the year 1 Reed prompted Moctezuma to consider that this light-skinned, bearded stranger who arrived from the east might indeed be Quetzalcoatl returning, as promised in legend, to reclaim his kingdom. In Tenochtitlan, Moctezuma consulted with his priests and soothsayers and offered incense and prayers to the gods. Was his throne truly threatened by a vengeful deity? The coincidence of dates plagued Moctezuma and he wavered in his assessment of how to treat the invaders—uncertain if they were gods to be appeased or mortal enemies to be opposed in war.

While Moctezuma vacillated, Cortés used the time to great advantage. With a group of his men, Cortés made forays into the countryside. At the Totonac capital of Cempoala the Spanish were warmly welcomed with wreaths of flowers. Again Cortés was given gifts, including eight noblewomen, to strengthen his relationship with the ruler of this rich center. From Cempoala the Spanish marched to the town of Quiahuiztlan, where they first encountered Moctezuma's despised and haughty tribute collectors. The unexpected arrival of these representatives of the emperor was greeted with fear and trembling by the Totonac ruler and his nobles. But Cortés boldly imprisoned the unwelcome visitors, thereby winning the alarmed Totonacs to his cause.

With his appetite for gold whetted by Moctezuma's rich and tantalizing gifts, Cortés began planning his march to the Aztec capital. With the help of Doña Marina, now fully allied with the Spanish cause, Cortés contacted local chiefs in the area and in a short time grew to understand the complicated politics of the Aztec world and the unrest and rebellion that underlay Moctezuma's oppressive regime.

In early summer 1519, the Spanish completed building the settlement of La Villa Rica de la Vera Cruz and, to validate his position in Mexico, Cortés had himself elected captain general and chief magistrate of the small town. On the basis of this new authority, Cortés disregarded Velásquez's claims and sent directly to Charles V, Holy Roman Emperor and Spain's new young king, most of the gold and treasure that had been collected so far on the expedition. With the ship went the first of his five letters to the king defending his actions in the New World.

VALLEY OF MEXICO

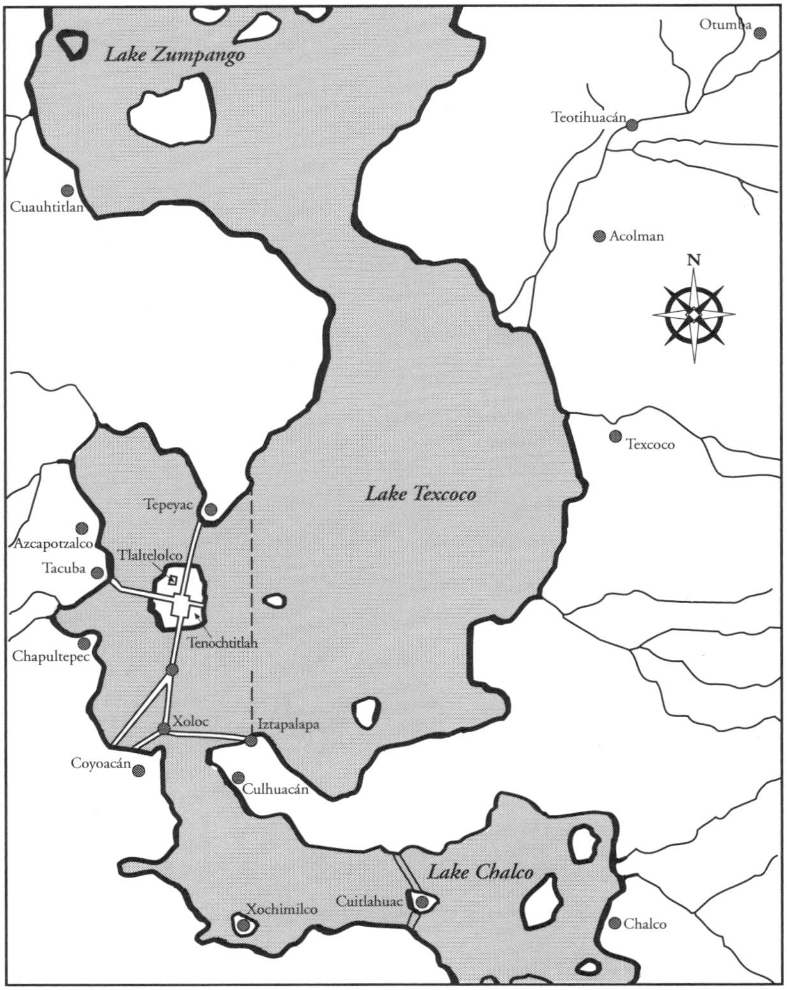

Finally, in July 1519, Cortés was ready to begin the dangerous trip to the heart of Mexico. To commit his wavering troops to the venture, Cortés sank four of his ships in the bay at Veracruz, and after removing useful gear, arms, and provisions, beached another six. This bold maneuver blocked a threatened rebellion of his men who, intimidated by the immensity of Mexico and the threat of its powerful ruler, wanted to abandon the endeavor and return to Cuba. By eliminating their only means of escape, Cortés ensured his troops' participation in his daring plan. Cortés chose one hundred fifty men to remain behind to protect the fledgling settlement of Veracruz. With the rest of his small army, Cortés once again departed for Cempoala. At this first major stop on his route to Tenochtitlan, Cortés hoped to obtain warriors

Map labels: Lake Zumpango, Otumba, Teotihuacán, Cuauhtitlan, Acolman, N, Texcoco, Lake Texcoco, Tepeyac, Azcapotzalco, Tlaltelolco, Tacuba, Tenochtitlan, Chapultepec, Xoloc, Iztapalapa, Coyoacán, Culhuacán, Lake Chalco, Xochimilco, Cuitlahuac, Chalco

from his new Totonac allies and native bearers to carry supplies.

During this second visit to Cempoala, Father Olmedo preached to the Indians and attempted to explain the tenets of Christianity and the Catholic faith, but to no avail. Finally, with the help of the Spanish soldiers, the priest threw the pagan idols from their position of honor atop the main pyramid and scrubbed the blood of sacrifice from the temple walls. A cross and altar were erected in their place. This action was repeated time and again as the Spanish usurped the most sacred places in the Aztec world to impose their own god and his symbols.

On August 16, 1519, with 400 Spaniards, 15 horses, 3 small guns, and 300 Indian warriors and porters, Cortés left Cempoala for Tenochtitlan. The journey led from the hot gulf lowlands, northwest to the mountain town of Jalapa, and then west over the high peaks of the coastal range. On his descent onto the plains near Tlaxcala, Cortés encountered the fierce warriors of the Tlaxcalan chiefs, traditional enemies of the Aztecs. Cortés and his men immediately became engaged in some of the toughest military action of the campaign. Carrying their ancestral banner depicting a great white heron, the men of Tlaxcala fought valiantly, mounting foray after foray against the Spanish forces. Throughout the desperate series of battles, Doña Marina encouraged the Spanish soldiers and tended their wounds, making herself loved by all, according to the chronicler Bernal Díaz. Finally, Spanish military prowess combined with deft diplomacy convinced the bellicose Tlaxcalan warriors to cast their lot with Cortés. On September 18, led by their chief Xicotencatl, the Tlaxcalan leaders, weary of the heavy Aztec tribute load and eager for revenge, committed their forces and destiny to the Spanish cause. Word of this significant alliance and of the Spanish military might was swiftly carried to Moctezuma by his ubiquitous spies and couriers.

The first joint battle of the Spanish and Tlaxcalan forces was at the ancient city of Cholula. On entering this traditional religious center, Cholulans escorted Cortés and his men to quarters near the central plaza. There, the wife of a local chief confided to Doña Marina that the Cholulans had been instructed by Moctezuma's messengers to ambush the Spaniards and carry them captive to the emperor. Doña Marina conveyed the information to Cortés, who cross-examined the cacique's wife, two priests, and finally the Aztec ambassadors themselves. All confirmed Doña Marina's story. In retaliation, Cortés called together the Cholulan rulers and their people in the great central plaza, had his men block the entrances, and then ordered his army to open fire. More than 3,000 men, women, and children were killed in the ensuing massacre. Messengers soon reported the bloodshed to Moctezuma, who, from his throne in Tenochtitlan, was fearfully monitoring the progress of the Spanish army. Moctezuma again sent gifts and messages to the Spanish, still hoping to discourage them from continuing to the capital. Cortés talked with these envoys through his translator, Doña Marina, and sent them back to tell a bewildered and uncertain Moctezuma that he would soon be in Tenochtitlan and was eager to meet the emperor.

Cortés pushed on, climbing with his soldiers and horses the high pass between Cholula and the Valley of Mexico. Crossing the snows of the last great mountain barrier, he wound his way down into the rich Mexican plateau. By this time his entourage consisted of 3,000 Tlaxcalan warriors and about 350 remaining Spanish soldiers. Wary of a surprise attack from the warriors of Moctezuma, the troops made their way cautiously into the heartland of the Aztecs, sleeping fully clothed with weapons at hand. Although Cortés's men often saw Aztec forces in the distance, none approached, and the army arrived safely at the city of Ixtapalapa on the southern edge of Lake Texcoco. There, Prince Cuitlahuac, kinsman of Moctezuma and lord of the city, greeted Cortés and provided spacious lodgings for his army.

From Ixtapalapa the Spanish had their first view of the splendid Aztec capital of Tenochtitlan. Bernal Díaz recorded the impact of that fantastic view across Lake Texcoco:

> And when we saw all those cities and villages built in the water,
> and other great towns on dry land, and that straight and level
> causeway leading to Mexico, we were astounded. These great
> towns and *cues* [temples] and buildings rising from the water, all
> made of stone, seemed like an enchanted vision . . . Indeed,
> some of our soldiers asked whether it was not all a dream. . . . It
> was all so wonderful . . . this first glimpse of things never heard
> of, seen or dreamed before.[5]

The seasoned Spanish soldiers who accompanied Cortés were astounded by the beauty and size of the city. They gazed in wonder at its gardens, palaces, pyramids, and magnificent temples rising from the shallow waters of Lake Texcoco into the clear blue sky of the high plateau.

The next morning, November 8, 1519, the Spanish captain Hernán Cortés and the Aztec ruler Moctezuma II met on a causeway approaching the island-capital of Tenochtitlan. The nobles of the Aztec empire, wearing sandals and elaborate finery, arrived first to announce the approach of the emperor. Then, with the eyes of all his subjects averted (a mandatory gesture of respect), Moctezuma himself was carried onto the causeway in a litter borne by eight of his chiefs. Cortés waited anxiously, with his captains and Doña Marina. The meeting was a momentous encounter of two worlds, generating fear, apprehension, and excitement on both sides.

> When Cortés saw . . . that the great [Moctezuma] was approaching, he dismounted from his horse, and when he came near to [Moctezuma] each bowed deeply to the other. [Moctezuma] welcomed our Captain and Cortés, speaking through Doña Marina, answered by wishing him very good health. Cortés . . . offered [Moctezuma] his right hand, but [Moctezuma] refused it and extended his own.[6]

As the Spanish and Tlaxcalan soldiers watched from the causeway, and the populace of Tenochtitlan observed the events from the rooftops of houses and from canoes on the lake, Moctezuma greeted Cortés:

> O our lord, thou hast suffered fatigue, thou hast endured weariness. Thou hast come to arrive on earth. Thou hast come to govern thy city of Mexico . . . which for a moment I have watched for thee, which I have guarded for thee.[7]

With these words the emperor seemed to welcome the returning Quetzalcoatl home. Moctezuma then had the soldiers and their captain escorted to the heart of the city, where he housed them, along with their horses, in the splendid palace of Axayacatl, his deceased father. The Spanish, incredibly, had become the honored guests of Moctezuma. Intent as always on finding gold, the soldiers immediately searched the luxurious palace for treasure. Behind a wall in the great dwelling they discovered a magnificent cache of gold ornaments made in the form of flowers, animals, and people. Without any opposition from the emperor, the Spaniards plundered and divided these treasures among themselves.

Moctezuma seemed drawn to Cortés, although whether as conqueror or god is uncertain. With Doña Marina translating, the two men held long conversations, hunted together in the emperor's private preserve, and toured the city. On one occasion Moctezuma escorted Cortés to the top of the great pyramid in the marketplace at Tlatelolco. There, from in front of the temple to Huitzilopochtli, Moctezuma pointed out the various neighborhoods of the capital, each with its own magnificent markets, palaces, and temples.

At first the Spanish professed friendship for their host, who so graciously provided them with living quarters, food, water, and servants. But as tension began to build among the populace of the vast capital, the Spanish became fearful that the emperor might turn and lead his people against them. Only a week after their arrival in Tenochtitlan, Cortés and his soldiers arrested Moctezuma and held him prisoner, a hostage to guarantee the good behavior of his subjects.

Moctezuma seemed resigned to his captivity. Even when several princes of the realm, led by the emperor's nephew Cacama, tried to rouse him to resist the invaders, he refused. While gathered in a secret meeting near Texcoco, these proud nobles from royal houses around the lake were arrested by order of Cortés, and imprisoned in Tenochtitlan. There, with arrogant and haughty demeanor, the Aztec nobles defiantly addressed the Spanish captains and accused their emperor of being unworthy of the proud lineage from which he was descended.

With the capture of these rebellious chiefs, Cortés felt secure enough to demand from Moctezuma a formal recognition of the supremacy of the Spanish king, Charles V. As in all other things, Moctezuma acquiesced. Calling the nobility of the empire together he proclaimed to them:

You will please me by giving yourselves to this captain as vassals
of the Emperor and King of Spain, our sovereign lord, to whom
I have already submitted as his servant and friend. And I implore
you to obey him henceforth, as you have obeyed me. . . .[8]

With these words the semidivine Moctezuma Xocoyotzin abdicated his position of supreme power.

Then an unforeseen event occurred. Cortés received word that Governor Velásquez had sent an expedition from Cuba. Led by Panfilo de Narvaez, its mission was to capture the renegade Cortés and take control of the conquest in Velásquez's name. Cortés hurried eastward to confront Narvaez, leaving his trusted captain Pedro Alvarado in charge of an apparently peaceful Tenochtitlan. Lured by the prospects of gold and glory, many of Narvaez's soldiers deserted to join Cortés, and Cortés emerged victorious from the skirmish. But at the end of the battle, Cortés received a desperate message from Alvarado, urging his immediate return to Tenochtitlan to rescue the Spanish garrison now under siege in their palace quarters.

Entering the capital on June 24, 1520, Cortés made his way through the restless city to Spanish headquarters. He soon learned that Alvarado had defied his orders to keep peace in the city. Alvarado had chosen the great Aztec festival of Toxcatl to massacre the bravest Aztec warriors and other celebrants as they danced in the sacred precinct to honor the god Huitzilopochtli. The Spanish soldiers "attacked all the celebrants, stabbing them, spearing them, striking them with their swords. . . . The blood of the warriors flowed like water and gathered into pools."[9]

The horror of the massacre drove the citizens of Tenochtitlan to rise up against the Spanish. With stones, slings, and arrows, the Aztecs drove the Spanish and their Tlaxcalan allies back into the palace of Ayaxacatl, to which they laid siege, permitting no food or water to pass. Cortés could not suppress his anger with Alvarado. The work of the last eight months seemed almost destroyed, but punishment had to be forgotten. In this moment of peril, Cortés needed all of his resources, including the impetuous captain.

Resentful of Moctezuma's policy of appeasement, the people of Tenochtitlan finally repudiated their emperor and chose as their military commander his younger brother Cuitlahuac. The powerful Aztec priests encouraged the rebellion, urging the people to defend their ancient deities and repulse the foreign invaders. The siege and attacks on the Spanish grew daily more intense; the Aztecs nearly succeeded in scaling the walls of the palace. In desperation, Cortés and his men tried once more to use Moctezuma's influence to calm his people. They lifted the emperor onto the battlements of the besieged fortress and Moctezuma attempted to speak to the angry crowd. At first they seemed to listen to their emperor's pleas for peace, but soon a barrage of stones and arrows was loosed at the barricades. Moctezuma fell, severely wounded. He refused to have his wounds tended or to take nourishment. Within three days the great emperor was dead. According to Bernal Díaz, Moctezuma's body was placed on a litter, and

> Cortés ordered six Mexicans, all important men . . . to carry him
> out on their shoulders and hand him over to the Mexican cap-
> tains . . . and they told Cuitlahuac . . . that his own people had
> killed the prince with three stones.[10]

CORTÉS

Moctezuma's death further inflamed the city. Under the leadership of Cuitlahuac, Aztec warriors occupied the Templo Mayor. From its high platforms overlooking Axayacatl's palace, Aztec warriors continuously attacked the Spanish quarters. Cortés could not allow the Aztecs to hold this natural fortress so he personally led a frontal attack up the great double stairway. The bloody skirmish ended with the Aztecs defeated, their bodies thrown down the stairs. But Cortés knew that, in spite of this victory, he was outnumbered and could not win the larger battle. After a sleepless night of deliberation, he called a council of his officers, and devised a plan to flee the city. Under the cover of darkness, the army would leave Tenochtitlan by means of the Tacuba causeway, using a mobile bridge to cross the canals where the bridges had been destroyed by the Aztecs.

On the night of June 30, 1520, the Spanish soldiers and their Tlaxcalan allies, weighted down with all the gold and booty they could carry, fought their way out of the city. The battle was a terrible disaster, remembered by the Spanish as *la Noche Triste*, or night of sorrows. The Aztecs were waiting for the Spaniards and their Indian allies, hounding them at every turn from canoes in the lake. Thousands died. Many were killed by the arrows and lances of the Aztec warriors. Others drowned as they rushed to escape, weighted down by the heavy treasure they refused to leave behind. Still others were captured only to become victims on the sacrificial stone of the Templo Mayor. Bernal Díaz records that of the 1,300 Spanish soldiers (the ranks enlarged by the addition of Narvaez's men), more than 860 died on that terrible night, along with half of the Tlaxcalan warriors. After this major victory, the Aztecs could easily have pursued and killed their enemies, but having put the Spanish and Tlaxcalans to flight, the Aztecs followed them only as far as Otumba, on the east side of the lake, then allowed Cortés and his forces to retreat over the mountains back to Tlaxcala. There, on July 11, Cortés's depleted and bedraggled troops were welcomed by the chief, Maxixca, and given refuge.

In Tenochtitlan the Aztecs crowned Cuitlahuac as their new emperor, and the capital returned to its normal daily and ritual life. Before long, however, the city was ravaged by a terrible plague of smallpox that had been carried to the New World by the Europeans. The inhabitants of the Americas had no immunity to this deadly disease and the epidemic killed many thousands of people, one of them the newly crowned king:

> The illness was so dreadful that no one could walk or move. The
> sick were so utterly helpless that they could only lie on their beds
> like corpses, unable to move . . . A great many died from this
> plague, and many others died of hunger. They could not get up
> to search for food, and everyone else was too sick to care for
> them, so they starved to death in their beds.[11]

Following the death of Cuitlahuac, a new emperor was selected. Cuauhtemoc, a cousin of Moctezuma, became the final defender and ruler of the fading Aztec empire.

For almost six months, Cortés and his men remained in Tlaxcala, strengthening their forces with additional Indian allies and Spanish soldier-adventurers newly arrived from Cuba, Jamaica, and Spain. In spite of the misfortunes of the initial invasion of Tenochtitlan, the Spaniards, their appetite whetted by thoughts of gold, pledged themselves to another attempt to capture the city. Cortés began preparing for the upcoming battle. While he and his forces subdued a number of Aztec-allied towns in the vicinity, Tlaxcalan craftsmen, under Spanish supervision, cut timber and planks

to build a fleet of thirteen small sailing ships. These ships, designed to maneuver in the shallow waters of Lake Texcoco, were to be used during the siege of the city. On December 28, 1520, with Indian porters carrying supplies and pulling the cannon, the Spanish soldiers marched back across the high mountain passes, down into the Valley of Mexico.

Cortés now had at his command a large army of Tlaxcalan warriors, new recruits from Spain and the Indies, plus his remaining veteran soldiers. With these forces, Cortés gained control of cities around the lake, beginning with the large town of Texcoco. In this important city, which controlled access to the lake and the passes out of the Valley, Cortés later installed as king, Ixtlilxochitl, a warrior-prince who proved to be a strong ally in the battle for Tenochtitlan. One after another the lakeshore towns surrendered. With the hinterlands secured, Cortés began his preparations to take the Aztec capital.

Anticipating the coming attack, Cuauhtemoc gathered a large army in the city. But in spite of heavy resistance by these Aztec forces, Cortés established his headquarters at the edge of the lake. There, the thirteen brigantines were assembled from the components carried across the mountains. On April 28, 1521, the small ships were launched on the shallow waters of Lake Texcoco. This fleet, armed with cannon, proved a major factor in the battle for the island-city. They were an almost invincible weapon against the wooden canoes of Tenochtitlan. An Aztec eyewitness reported:

> The cannons were fired into the thick of the flotilla, wherever the canoes were crowded closest together. Many of our warriors were killed outright; others drowned because they were too crippled by their wounds to swim away. The water was red with the blood of the dead and dying.[12]

Cortés's plan was to blockade the city and, by securing and controlling the causeways leading from the mainland, cut off all supplies and aid.

On May 31, 1521, the siege of Tenochtitlan began. One of the major Spanish objectives was to drive the Aztec canoes and warriors back into Tenochtitlan, so the canals and gaps in the causeways could be filled in with rubble to allow horsemen and soldiers access to the capital from the mainland. Battle after battle ensued, with Cuauhtemoc sending his forces at night to clear the canals filled in by the Spanish during the day. The fighting was ferocious; many on both sides were wounded or killed. At the end of the day, from their camps at the edge of the lake, the Spanish soldiers would hear the mournful shell trumpets sound from the Templo Mayor and watch in horror as their captured comrades were dragged up the pyramid steps to be offered as sacrifices to the Aztec gods.

Working feverishly, Cortés's army finally filled the gaps in the causeways and Spanish soldiers and cavalry, along with as many as 150,000 Indian allies, poured into the city. The Spanish, determined to avoid capture (and death by sacrifice), fought with abandon. At the same time, the fierce Tlaxcalan warriors took every opportunity for bloody revenge on their traditional Aztec enemies. Yet over and over again, the Spaniards and Tlaxcalans were driven back by the Aztec army, led by Cuauhtemoc and his great captain Tzilacatzin. Uncontrolled butchery and killing ensued on both sides as the Spanish secured the city, street by street, through bitter hand-to-hand combat.

The blockade imposed by the invaders caused great anguish as the capital became more and more decimated by disease and the lack of food and fresh water. The final battle for Tenochtitlan was fought in the imposing marketplace of Tlatelolco. There Cuauhtemoc, his nobles, and warriors made a last valiant stand for their city. But the forces of the Spanish and their native allies were too powerful. The fall of Tenochtitlan came on August 13, 1521. The siege had lasted 74 days. Of the 300,000 warriors who had defended the capital, only 60,000 were left.

The heroic young ruler Cuauhtemoc attempted to flee the city by canoe, but was soon captured and brought before Cortés. Bernal Díaz records the words he spoke to the Spanish captain:

> "I have assuredly done my duty in defence of my city and my vassals, and I can do no more. I am brought by force as a prisoner into your presence . . . Take the dagger that you have in your belt, and strike me dead immediately."[13]

Cortés did not comply with Cuauhtemoc's plea. Instead, he imprisoned the emperor and his family in the lakeside town of Coyocan and allowed the starving remnants of the population to evacuate the devastated city. For three days men, women, and children streamed along the causeways to the mainland. Their sorrow is revealed in the words of an Aztec poem:

> Our cries of Grief rise up
> and our tears rain down,
> for Tlatelolco is lost.
> . . . .
> The walls are black,
> the air is black with smoke,
> the guns flash in the darkness.
> They have captured Cuauhtemoc;
> they have captured the princes of Mexico.[14]

The Aztec empire had fallen. The glorious city of Tenochtitlan was destroyed. Neither the New World nor the Old would ever be the same again.

Once the city was secured, the Spanish troops celebrated the victorious conclusion of the long, laborious campaign with a wild and rowdy banquet that lasted through the night. But as soon as the celebrants returned to their senses, their major concern was the search for gold. The soldiers were convinced that the emperor and his nobles had hidden a rich trove of Aztec treasure somewhere in the city, but they were unable to discover its location. Cuauhtemoc and his chiefs were questioned again and again. Finally, with the permission of Cortés and with the priests as witnesses, Cuauhtemoc and the ruler of Tacuba were tortured by having their feet held to a fire.

In spite of their pain and humiliation, the defeated rulers responded by saying only that most of the gold had been thrown into the lake.

But the Spanish never stopped hungering for treasure, plundering what they did find and fighting for possession of it among themselves. Soon after the fall of Tenochtitlan, this thirst for gold led the Spaniards on routes of conquest throughout the Aztec empire. In October 1524, Cortés himself set out for Honduras in search of treasure, heading off a possible uprising during his absence by taking along the captive emperor Cuauhtemoc. The journey was long and arduous; Cortés was in constant fear that Cuauhtemoc might provide a rallying point for a native rebellion. Deep in the jungles of Campeche, Cortés found an opportunity to dispose of the troublesome ruler. Falsely accusing Cuauhtemoc of insurrection, Cortés had the emperor hanged. Even Gómara, Cortés's biographer, said of the execution:

> Cortés, indeed, should have preserved his life as a precious jewel,
> for Cuauhtémoc was the triumph and glory of his victories; but
> Cortés did not wish to keep him alive in such a troubled land
> and time.[15]

With the death of Cuauhtemoc the final chapter had been written. The glory of Tenochtitlan and the Aztec world had truly vanished in the final fury and flame of conquest.

THE AFTERMATH

Although Cortés and his comrades lusted for fortune, the aesthetic beauty of the gold ornaments fashioned by Aztec artists held little interest for them. Most of the magnificent pieces were purposely tossed into crucibles, melted into bubbling golden liquid, and cast into ingots of standardized weight. From these, the king's "fifth" was carefully set aside for the coffers of Charles V of Spain. As a result, only a handful of the splendid objects described by the chroniclers remain today. The bars of gold, along with carefully selected examples of the Aztecs' finest jewelry, were sent by ship to Spain, where they were displayed with great pomp at three royal courts of the empire. In Seville, Valladolid, and Brussels, the splendor of Moctezuma's gifts to Cortés and the plundered golden treasure of the Aztecs, dazzled the world of Renaissance Europe.

Fortune hunting exploded in Spain. Soon adventurers, priests, bureaucrats, and soldiers flocked to New Spain (Mexico) in search of fame, riches, and converts to Catholicism. A few came to make Mexico their home or to enlighten Indian souls, but most came simply to pillage the wealth of the new land. For almost three hundred years the Aztecs and other indigenous peoples languished under the colonial yoke of Spain. Finally in 1821, revolution broke the bonds that tied New Spain to Europe, and Mexico rose as an independent country. Today, in modern Mexico, a powerful national identity blends the genetic and cultural heritage of the Old and New Worlds in an innovative tradition unique to the Americas.

Notes

1. Francisco López de Gómara, Cortéz: *The Life of the Conqueror by His Secretary*, trans. and ed. L.B. Simpson (Berkeley, 1964), p. 25.

2. *Cantares Mexicanos*, fol. 19 v.–20 r. in Miguel León-Portilla, *Pre-Columbian Literatures of Mexico*, trans. G. Lobanov (Norman, 1969), p. 87.

3. Bernal Díaz del Castillo, *The Conquest of New Spain*, trans. J.M. Cohen (Baltimore, 1963), pp. 224–25.

4. Díaz del Castillo, *The Conquest of New Spain*, p. 93.

5. Díaz del Castillo, *The Conquest of New Spain*, p. 214.

6. Díaz del Castillo, *The Conquest of New Spain*, p. 217.

7. Fray Bernardino de Sahagún, *Florentine Codex: General History of the Things of New Spain*, trans. A.J.O. Anderson and C.E. Dibble (Santa Fe and Salt Lake City, 1950–1982), Book 12, chap.16, p. 44.

8. Gómara, *Cortez: The Life of the Conqueror by His Secretary*, p. 185.

9. Miguel León-Portilla, *The Broken Spears*, trans. L. Kemp (Boston, 1962), p. 76.

10. Díaz del Castillo, *The Conquest of New Spain*, p. 295.

11. León-Portilla, *The Broken Spears*, p. 93.

12. León-Portilla, *The Broken Spears*, p. 96.

13. Díaz del Castillo, *The Conquest of New Spain*, p. 403.

14. *Cantares Mexicanos*, fol. ss v.–r. in León-Portilla, *The Broken Spears*, p. 146–148.

15. Gómara, *Cortez: The Life of the Conqueror by His Secretary*, p. 356.

SELECTED BIBLIOGRAPHY

Anonymous Conqueror. "Relacion de alguna cosas de las Nueva España y de la Gran Ciudad de Temestitan Mexico." *Coleccion de Documentos para la Historia de Mexico*, Vol. 1. ed. J.C. Icazbalceta. Editorial Porrua, 1971.

Berdan, Frances. *The Aztecs of Central Mexico: An Imperial Society*. New York: Holt, Rinehart and Winston, 1982.

Cortés, Hernándo. *Hernándo Cortés: Five Letters 1519–1526*. trans. J. Bayard Morris. New York: W.W. Norton, 1969.

Davies, Nigel. *The Aztecs*. New York: Putnam,1974.

Díaz del Castillo, Bernal. *The Conquest of New Spain*. trans. J.M. Cohen. Baltimore: Penguin, 1963.

Durán, Fray Diego. *The Book of the Gods and The Ancient Calendar*. trans. and ed. Doris Heyden and Fernando Horcasitas. Norman: University of Oklahoma Press, 1971.

Gómara, Francisco López de. *Cortés: The Life of the Conqueror by His Secretary*. trans. and ed. L.B. Simpson. Berkeley and Los Angeles: University of California Press, 1964.

León-Portilla, Miguel. *Aztec Thought and Culture: A Study of the Ancient Nahuatl Mind.* trans. Jack Emory Davis. Norman: University of Oklahoma Press, 1963.

———. *The Broken Spears.* English trans. Lysander Kemp. Boston: Beacon Press, 1966.

———. *Pre-Columbian Literatures of Mexico.* trans. Grace Lobanov and the author. Norman: University of Oklahoma Press, 1969.

Nicholson, Keith. "The Artist and the Book—Conversations with Keith Henderson." *Antiquarian Book Monthly Review,* Vol. 2, No. 11. (1975), pp. 18–28.

Prescott, William H. *The Conquest of Mexico.* Illustrations by Keith Henderson and with an introduction by T.A. Joyce. New York: Henry Holt and Company; and London: Chatto & Windus, 1922.

———. *The Conquest of Mexico.* Illustrated by Keith Henderson and with an introduction by Carl Van Doren. New York: The Junior Literary Guild, 1934.

Sahagún, Fray Bernardino de. *Florentine Codex: General History of the Things of New Spain.* trans. Arthur J.O. Anderson and Charles E. Dibble. Santa Fe and Salt Lake City: The School of American Research and the University of Utah, 1950–1982.

Soustelle, Jacques. *Daily Life of the Aztecs on the Eve of the Spanish Conquest.* trans. Patrick O'Brian. Harmondsworth: Penguin Books, Ltd., 1961.

Wagner, Henry R. *The Rise of Fernando Cortes: Documents and Narratives Concerning the Discovery and Conquest of Latin America.* Berkeley: The Cortés Society, Bancroft Library, California. 1944.

PART II

THE DRAWINGS OF KEITH HENDERSON

At age nineteen, Cortés sailed from Spain to the New World in a
convoy of merchant ships bound for Santo Domingo.

When Cortés arrived in Santo Domingo, he registered as a citizen of the colony,
which entitled him to a building plot and land for cultivation.

At age thirty-four, Cortés led an expedition to Mexico from the Spanish
island of Cuba in search of gold, glory, and souls.

As his ships made their way up the gulf coast of Mexico, Cortés and his men
paused to trade in local Indian towns.

The Spanish heard from the natives of the rich Aztec empire
and its powerful ruler, Moctezuma II.

At the Maya city of Potonchán, the Spanish cavalry charged
into battle against a strong force of hostile Indians.

Marina was a bright and beautiful young Indian girl. She was presented
as a gift to Cortés from the chief of Potonchán.

Kneeling in the sand, Spanish soldiers and Indians offered thanks for their safe arrival at the future site of Veracruz.

The priest-soldier Father Olmedo gave a sermon to the Spanish forces.

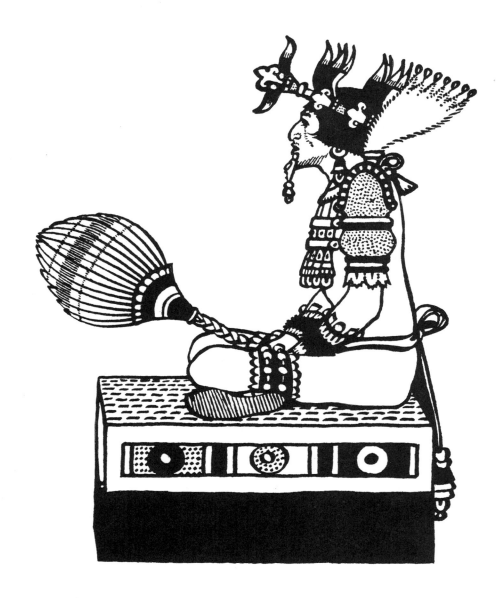

Moctezuma Xocoyotzin was the absolute ruler of the powerful Aztec state.

Moctezuma's many wives and concubines lived in special quarters
within the palace in the city of Tenochtitlan.

Moctezuma's elaborate meals included foods
brought from all regions of the empire.

The emperor's dinner ended with a rich drink of
frothing chocolate served in a golden cup.

Dancers entertained the emperor.

Musicians provided entertainment while Moctezuma dined.

Was Cortés the returning god-king Quetzalcoatl? Moctezuma sought the answer by consulting with his priests and offering incense and prayers to the gods.

Doña Marina quickly learned Spanish and allied herself
with Cortés as his translator and mistress.

In the large town of Cempoala, the natives welcomed Cortés
and his men with gifts and wreaths of flowers.

Cortés was given eight noblewomen to strengthen his
relationship with the ruler of Cempoala.

At Quiahuiztlan, the Spanish made their first contact with Moctezuma's despised and haughty tribute collectors.

With the help of the Spanish soldiers, Father Olmedo threw down the idols
from their honored position atop the main pyramid of Cempoala.

As Cortés and his men made their way inland, they encountered
the fierce warriors of the Tlaxcalan chiefs.

Carrying their ancestral banner depicting a great white heron, the warriors
of Tlaxcala fought valiantly again the Spanish forces.

Through a desperate series of battles with the Tlaxcalans, Doña Marina
encouraged the Spanish soldiers and tended their wounds.

Spies and couriers carried word of Spanish military prowess to Moctezuma
and reported that Cortés had formed an alliance with the Tlaxcalans.

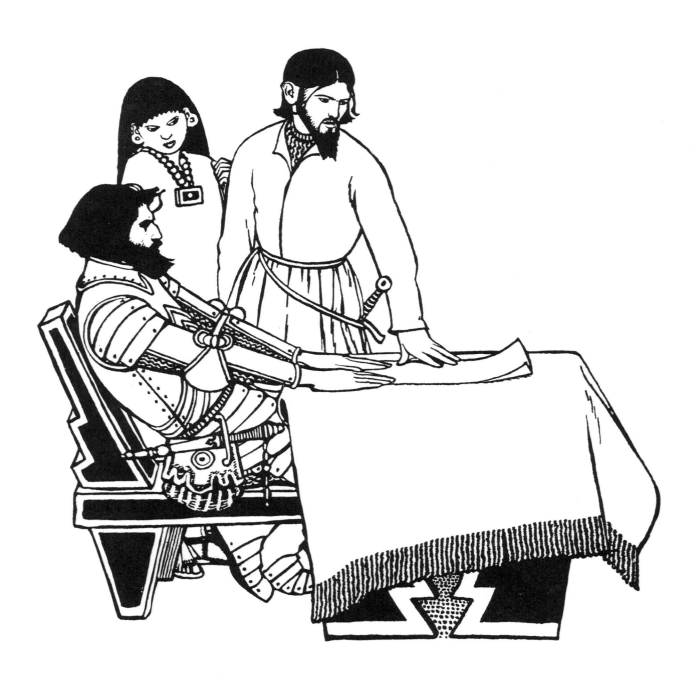

At Cholula, Cortés cross-examined the chief's wife about the plot against the Spanish.

Cortés questioned two Cholulan priests.

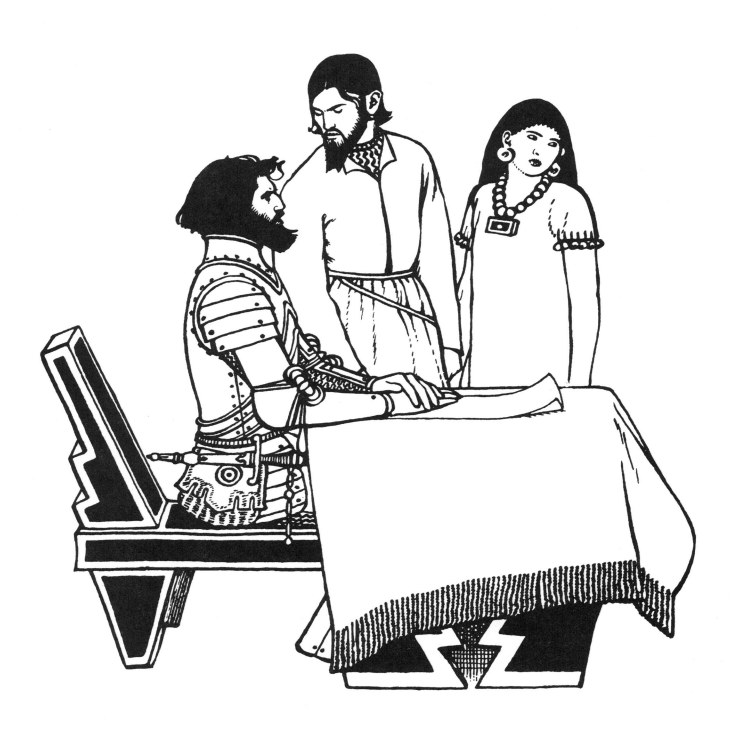

Cortés cross-examined the Aztec ambassadors about Moctezuma's scheme.

More than 3,000 men, women, and children were killed by Spanish and Tlaxcalan forces in the massacre at Cholula.

Moctezuma fearfully monitored the progress of the
Spanish from his Tenochtitlan throne.

On November 8, 1519, an elaborately dressed procession of Aztec nobles walked along the causeway from Tenochtitlan to announce the approach of the emperor.

Moctezuma II was carried from the city on a magnificent litter borne
by eight of his chiefs, as Spanish soldiers watched intently.

Moctezuma and Cortés bowed to each other in greeting.

It was a momentous encounter of two worlds with fear,
apprehension, and excitement on both sides.

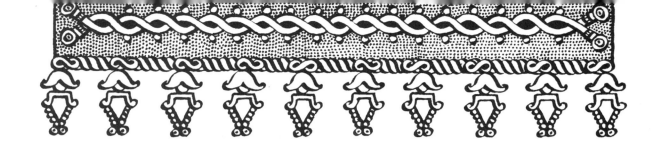

With Doña Marina translating, Cortés and Moctezuma held long conversations.

From on top of a great pyramid, Moctezuma showed Cortés
the magnificent city of Tenochtitlan.

After only a week in Tenochtitlan, Cortés and his soldiers arrested Moctezuma.

The Spanish feared the emperor might turn and lead his people against them.

The Spanish held Moctezuma as a hostage to guarantee
the good behavior of his subjects.

Without success the Aztec prince Cacama tried to rouse
the emperor to resist the Spanish invaders.

Captured by Cortés's soldiers, Prince Cacama defied the Spanish captains
with his arrogant and haughty demeanor.

Cortés forced the semidivine emperor Moctezuma II
to abdicate his position of supreme power.

After the Spanish massacre of Aztec warriors at the Templo Mayor, Cortés
could not suppress his anger over the actions of Alvarado.

The people of Tenochtitlan finally repudiated Moctezuma and chose
as their military leader his younger brother, Cuitlahuac.

The powerful Aztec priests encouraged revolt in the city, urging
the people to defend their ancient gods.

Spiraling smoke signaled the Aztecs' preparations for war.

Aztec attacks on the Spanish forces grew daily more intense.

The Aztecs nearly succeeded in scaling the walls
of the palace fortress held by the Spanish.

Moctezuma stood on the battlements of the besieged palace
and spoke to the angry crowd.

The Aztecs turned against Moctezuma and loosed a barrage of stones and arrows.
The emperor fell, severely wounded.

Moctezuma refused to have his wounds treated or to take nourishment.
Within three days the great emperor was dead.

Moctezuma's lifeless body was placed on a litter and carried out of the Spanish quarters.
The Aztec chiefs presented the body to Cuitlahuac, Moctezuma's younger brother.

During the ensuing battles, Cortés personally led a frontal attack against the Aztecs, charging up the double stairway of the great pyramid.

After deliberating the serious situation the Spanish faced in Tenochtitlan, Cortés
called a council of his officers and devised a plan to flee the city.

On July 10, 1520, the Spanish and their Tlaxcalan allies, weighted down with booty,
fought their way out of the city.

The flight was a terrible disaster for the Spanish, still remembered as
la Noche Triste, or the night of sorrows.

The Spanish retreated to Tlaxcala, where they were welcomed by Chief Maxixca.

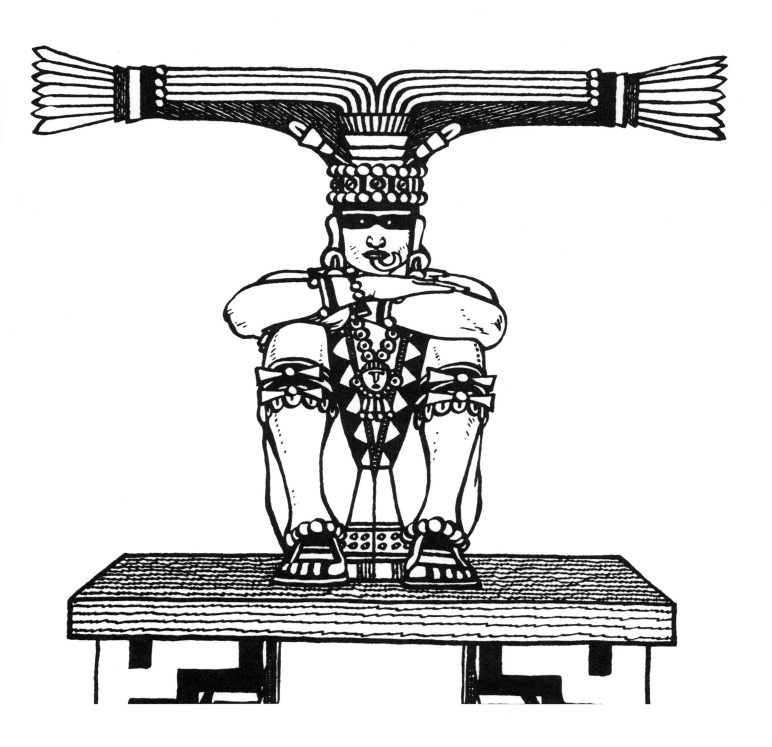

In Tenochtitlan, the Aztecs crowned Cuitlahuac as the new emperor.

Upon the death of Cuitlahuac in the first great plague of smallpox, Moctezuma's nephew Cuauhtemoc was selected to rule the fading Aztec empire.

Still dreaming of gold and glory, the Spanish soldiers pledged themselves
to another attempt to capture Tenochtitlan.

The Aztec warriors of the emperor Cuauhtemoc mounted heavy
resistance against the Spanish forces.

Under cover of night, Cuauhtemoc sent his forces to battle the Spanish
and destroy the causeways leading into the city.

The Spanish heard the mournful shell trumpets
sound from the great temple in Tenochtitlan

From their camp at the edge of the lake, the Spanish soldiers could see their captured comrades dragged up the pyramid steps to be sacrificed to the Aztec gods.

Uncontrolled killing and butchery occurred as the Spanish and their allies secured the city in bitter hand-to-hand combat.

Standing before Cortés, Cuauhtemoc spoke: "I have assuredly done my duty in defense of my city . . . I am brought by force as a prisoner into your presence . . . Take the dagger that you have in your belt, and strike me dead immediately."
(Bernal Díaz, 1963, p. 403)

With these passionate words, the last Aztec emperor surrendered to the Spanish and was taken as a prisoner to the town of Coyocan.

The Spanish troops celebrated the victorious conclusion of the
campaign with a wild and rowdy banquet.

Determined to learn the whereabouts of Aztec gold, the Spanish
tortured the emperor Cuauhtemoc.

On the pretext of conspiracy, Cortés had Cuauhtemoc hanged. With his death in 1525, the final chapter of the conquest was written.

Artist's Credits*

inside front cover: GREAT WHITE HERON *(Adea occidentalis).*

running footers: GREAT NORTHERN DIVERS *(Gavia immer).*

i: RATTLESNAKE. Codex Zouche, p. 79.

ii: RACCOONS *(Procyon lotor).*

iii: QUETZALS *(Pharomacrus mocinno).*

iv: SHORT-EARED OWL *(Asio flammeus).* The favourite birds of Mictlantecuhtli, god of death : sinister birds. See . . . the Codices Vaticanus B, p. 91; Bologna, p. 12; and Borgia, p. 18.

v: A STINGING INSECT. Codex Borgia, p. 27. Oviedo (Purchas, p. 164) describes such a creatures as "a little mischievous worm, which we may number among the kindes of Fleas."

iv: SPIDER MONKEY *(Ateles ater).*

vii: HUMMING-BIRD. See . . . Oviedo (Purchas, p. 168) who says, "This bird, beside her littlenesse, is of such velositie and swiftnesse in flying, that who so seeth her flying in the aire, cannot see her flap or beate her wings after any other sort than doe the humble Bees."

ix: PECCARY. *(Dicotyles).* See . . . the Codex Zouche, p. 73.

xi: SPIDER MONKEY *(Ateles ater).* See . . . the Codices Vaticanus B, p. 86; Borgia, p. 13; and Bodley, pp. 13, 32 (Kingsborough).

1: RABBIT *(Sylvilagus sp.).* Codex Borgia, p. 18. Oviedo (Purchas, p. 219) considered the Mexican rabbits as "liker Hares than Conies, yet less than Conies."

8: HUITZILOPOTCHTLI. Codex Borgia, p. 50. Notice the humming-birds, the huitzitzilin on his massive necklace.

9: RED AND BLUE MACAW *(Ara macao).* See . . . the Codex Selden, p. 7.

9: A FISHERMAN. Codex Vaticanus B, p. 32.

11: POSTHUMOUS PORTRAIT OF MOCTEZUMA IN HIS YOUTH AS AN ARMY OFFICER. His face is painted, the upper half yellow, the lower half red. Codex Vaticanus A, p. 128 (Kingsborough).

17: EAGER TO CATCH A GLIMPSE OF THE STRANGERS. See the Codex Mendoza, pp. 61, 64 (Kingsborough).

22–23: NATIVE *TAMANES* TO DRAG THE GUNS AND TRANSPORT THE BAGGAGE. See the Codex Mendoza, p. 63 (Kingsborough).

26: CROCODILE. Codices Laud, p. 14; Zouche, p. 75; and Fejérváry-Mayer, p. 4. The Laud crocodile is furnished with two nose-jewels and a headdress of feathers.

27: BLACK-WINGED STILT *(Himantopus mexicanus).*

28: JAGUAR *(Felis onca).* Codices Vaticanus B, p. 25; Zouche, pp. 24, 50; Borgia, p. 44; Laud, p. 22 (Kingsborough). "Terrible beasts," Oviedo writes (Purchas, pp. 206, 207), "in shape like unto a Tigre. Their bodies and their legs are full of black spots one neere unto another and divided with a circumference or fringe of reddish colour, showing, as it were, a faire work and correspondent picture."

30: EAGLES. See . . . the Codices Borgia, p. 20, and Zouche, p. 69.

inside back cover: JAGUARS [notes missing].

*Keith Henderson's notes on his drawings from the codices, adapted from "List of Illustrations with Notes by the Artist," in *The Conquest of Mexico*